this exquisite corpse

Tawnya Selene Renelle

CALENTUREPRESS

First published in Great Britain by Calenture Press

ISBN: 978-0-9575018-5-0

Printed and bound by Lightning Source

A catalogue record of this book is available from the British Library.

Typeset in Crimson and Elephant

Typesetting by Calenture Press.

Art on page 41 by Tina Testaverde. All photos by the very missed and loved Gitana Januszewski

Cover design by Claire Spinks and Cailean McBride. With kind thanks to Megspl (pomegranate) and SarahRichterArt (torn paper) for use of their images (via Pixaby.com) on the front cover.

To:

Grandmother: for words to write poems she won't read
Friends: for experiences worth writing about
Ylla: for spirit and insight
Cal and Colin: for believing in this book
Bhanu, Rebecca, and Bea: for strength, freedom, and
support

this exquisite corpse

Introduction: Reading Tawnya Renelle's Poems

A BOOK of deviance. A book of delight. An embodied book. A personal book. A book of family. A book of fetish. A book of memories and memorialising. A book, above all, of pleasure. This collection of poetry by Tawnya Renelle is all of these things. In disarming, radical excursions through sexuality, gender politics, familial bonds and relationships of all kinds, Renelle awakens (and sometimes rhythmically lulls) the insides and the outsides of our bodies with a language exquisitely attuned to the frequencies of now.

This is a provocative collection. Poetry this direct, this invested in its embodied experience, is always provocative. I'm reminded of Etel Adnan's remark that "subversion is the changing of the world." In Renelle's poems, you can practically feel the world's moistened changing, its vibratory pulsing transformation: "Face leaned against tub/ pants wet / shaking / beads of sweat"; "the orgasms you gave me / are still between my thighs". That shift from "-ts wet" to "sweat" – that's the changing of language and world together!

The poet June Jordan once asked "how do we come to be here next to each other / in the night". This question of adjacency, of how our bodies inhabit spaces in relation to other bodies, is just one of the questions that animates this collection. The poem 'Muscle Memory' enacts this in the enmeshing choreography of intimacy: "on the couch in the living room / my face between your legs". In 'our noises', Renelle attunes us to particular kinds of sounds - the sorts of sounds our bodies make while simultaneously receiving sound - "the slack drop of the body"; "the pounding / of water against shower wall". These sounds, both inside and outside, open up possibilities of deviant porousness, if only we follow Renelle's lead and hear them.

Elsewhere it's an image that encapsulates the frothy openness, sud-like desire and possibility. In Renelle's poem 'Wake Up', for example, there's "a washing machine overflowing with clothing / soap spilling onto my feet". This excessive, foaming, spilling of language is about the desire for radical forms of intimacy and relationality too. As Eileen Myles says "Foam means I want". Or as another Renelle poem puts it, "Sometimes I think too much".

Always, through its encounters with grief, break-up, loss, illness, addiction, self-examination, Renelle's language is buoyant, and dazzles, twists, turns in unexpected ways. The poems wrap and encompass with their alive-ness. One of the energies in the collection is to list, to "collect myself", to document, as a way of negotiating and orienting oneself in relation to the occurrences, objects, fabric of the world: "I know this list will never stop".

Tawnya Renelle's poetry is urgent, echoing and vibrant. Her images haunt, comfort and contort. This is a collection that as the feeling at its core unravels, pours forth, foams, agitates and spills, you won't want to stop.

Colin Herd
April 2019

this exquisite corpse

I

Alive

Conception

Nobody wants to think about their parents having sex

but I think about mine
because I wonder how my mom slept with a man who hit her.

Pregnancy

I asked my mom
   if she thought about aborting me.

An unplanned bastard

   What is the female word for Bastard?

Illegitimate

She told me it was never an option.

I think she might have lied, worried about hurting my feelings.

I would be proud to have been almost aborted,

that my mom had a choice.

Maybe it wasn't an option because I was hope.

A baby that might end violence

Birth

but I didn't.

I wonder about how much of a disappointment it was to her.

For Grandmother

I date women
I date men
I have always loved all people

but it doesn't change my love
for you to not know

Our bond is not dependent on your knowing

I do not believe in god
but I wonder what would happen if I did
Would the death of my friends make more sense?
Would I understand a plan?
     Would I find the peace   you want for me?

I will try to understand death someday on your terms
     when you die
          and will read the book you have
asked me to

I prayed to god as I drove to take you to the Emergency Room
I prayed because you believe in Him
I prayed because you believe

You worry about using a handicap placard that is not yours
I tell you not to worry because you have never committed a
crime

I have committed crimes

I have bought and sold drugs
I have stolen things

I have driven after drinking
I have vandalized
but

Our bond is not dependent on your knowing

I worked at Planned Parenthood
For three years of my life
I told you I worked at just a health clinic
I assisted with Medical abortions
I counseled patients about pregnancy options
I taught young women and men to become sexually
responsible
       The one time we talked about abortion
You cried   when I said I thought life does not begin
at conception

Our bond is not dependent on your knowing

I don't feel hidden
       or closeted
or ashamed
       or that I needed to

This bond is not dependent on your knowing

Inherited

Here is what I know:

Her father's nickname was Rusty.

She will not talk about her father.

Here is what I know:

Her father had red hair and was adopted.

She will not talk about her father.

Here is what I know:

My father had a red mustache.

I do not talk about my father.

My hair is red.

Here is what I know:

Her father was an alcoholic.

Her father refused to know her. (When she met him she was pregnant and unmarried.)

My father was angry: he hit, he yelled, he touched

She will not talk about her father.
She will not talk about her father.
        I do not talk about my father.

This is what I know.

Choked

and then I pulled my spine
out through my throat
flipped myself
inside out
and sewed my skin back together

Timeline

August 26th-4:45 PM: G pulled the trigger of a needle packed full of Heroin. She is Dead.

Day 1: My eyes open to the nightmare and the only feeling I have is the end of the needle of a tattoo gun that drives the word Gypsy into my skin.

Day 2: I drive, my eyes glued open with sorrow from Portland to Bellingham, the car smells of G. We have packed all her belongings. We are bringing them home.

Day 3: We plunge into the water, a wailing weeping group, but I cannot remember how to swim and I hope that I will drown.

Day 4: E drives back from Bellingham to Portland because I have not slept, because I do not understand hunger, but my body is shaking because it does.

Day 5: I am denied grief leave because she wasn't my sister by blood, I use the throat strength that remains to request all of my vacation time.

Day 8: I pull my body together so that I may hold up the bodies of others as I walk them one by one into the room of weeping and viewing. Her body does not move.

Day 11: A wedding was planned years in advance. I drive from Portland to Bellingham. I sit in stoned silence as G's boyfriend weeps next to me. I squeeze his hand.

Day 15: Jobs must be returned to, the world did not stop. My body feels dismantled.

Day 30: A familiar pain returns in my lower lumbar.

Day 45: I am granted medical leave. My body is now dismantled and broken.

Day 65: B drives from Portland to Bellingham because I cannot feel the bottom of my foot.

Day 67 *Day of the Dead:* Her memorial is held in a bar and my hand shakes as I place candy and chips on the altar.

Day 92: Emergency Magnetic Resonance Imaging, my body is broken. My spine shattered.

December 4th-6:00pm: A has shot himself in the head. I have held that gun. He is dead.

Day 2: I cry in bed because I cannot drive from Portland to Bellingham, my spine is broken.

Day 5: I go under the knife. My body cut and splayed open to heal. The foreign entrance of metal to mend the disc.

Day 15: I consume pain pills by the prescription directions as T drives from Portland to Bellingham, I will be home for Christmas.

Day 30: My body is dismantled. My spine is healing. I will not return to work. My body has changed the jobs I can do.

Day 45: My body feels dismantled. My heart is broken. There is no healing. I cannot stay.

Day 80: My spine is healing, protected by others who carry my heavy boxes into a uhaul.

Day 85: I drive from Portland to Bellingham. I move my dismantled body and broken heart. I drive in silence. Sometimes I still cannot feel the bottom of my right foot.

Day 365 August 26th: We spread G's ashes over the bridge at Deception pass. A line of 16 mourners, Dahlias in hands. I light a smoke and take a drag. I toss it to the water below.

Virginity

I had sex for the first time when I was 13

>   She was 14

Our mothers best friends
Our trailers side by side
>   in the park I can't remember the name of
>   on the street I can't remember the name of

Our mothers would sit chain smoking on the weekends
>   drinking coffee

Slumber parties weekly

Our mothers would move smoke-filled lungs
from outside to inside
wine coolers opened
ZZ Top and Stevie Ray Vaughn blaring out from the tape deck

>   Left alone we talked and laughed

Let's pretend one of us is the boy and one the girl
>   She told me
Do you have a pair of socks?

We opened the drawer full of colors, choosing 2 pairs

I'll be the boy first
>   She said
She removed her pants
and as I watched her shove the wad
into her purple flowered underwear
I felt something beneath my green and blue striped panties

9

The weight of her body on top of mine
our hips smashing
pressing the socks hard between us

Back and forth
Up and down

Her sock wad penis rubbed against my puberty engorged
vagina

When do we know when to stop?
        I asked

Up and down
Back and forth

Do you feel anything?
        She asked

Did I feel anything?

Between my legs warmth had turned to wetness
A pulsating
        A wetness

Yes
        I said

For two years we would have this sock stuffed romance
until she turned 16 and started having sex with boys

I wouldn't have sex with a boy till I was 20

Haunting

She has been broken and reset twice

every ache strain pain pinch pull

right above the butt
at the base in the middle

She has been broken and reset twice

She will face it as she ages
as she hikes
as she does dishes
as she has sex
as she drives
       if she has kids
       if she falls
       if she moves wrong

This broken disc will linger like a haunting

Grief

In bed together
I said
I wish she were alive
so I could tell her about us
You said
I wish he were alive too
and then silence

Muscle Memory

The orgasms you gave me
are still between my thighs

Now the places we have been
                    pound within me

I sit on the stairs to my bedroom
            fingers deep within you
                        your fingers deep within me

I sit on the green floral chair in the living room
            your face buried between my legs

On the couch in the living room
            my face between your legs

The front door of my apartment
            you pressed against it begging me for more

At my computer at work
            your words and my words and touching myself in the
bathroom

In the kitchen
            your hand slipping down my pants as I cook

The bed in my friend's cabin, the bed with sheep wool blankets
            our first moments of discovery

And my bed
            no night spent there together without

the orgasms you gave me

Hangover

There is no eating
when the whiskey of last night rumbles
        in the belly
a resurfacing
reversing
from mouth to esophagus to stomach

I am choking on the bile of last night's decisions

Breakfast

The taste of too many cigarettes

I gag and purge so hard I've peed my pants

I am choking on the bile of last night's decisions

Break
Fast

            Face leaned against tub
                pants wet
                        shaking
                                beads of sweat

We Have All Felt Like Fat Girls

Fat girls cry in the dressing room
in the mirror you squeeze into pants too tight
but you are just skin pulled over bone

Tears well in the corners of your eyes
you stare at the body hoping for a fight
Fat girls cry in the dressing room

Exacerbated you sit and sigh
sweating under your breasts from fluorescent light
but you are just skin pulled over bone

You cannot bear finding more to try
how did the vision of self become skewed sight
Fat girls cry in the dressing room

The mannequins outside the room smile a lie
winking as if they know what is right
but you are just skin pulled over the bone

You feel like when they measured fat in junior high
remember outside of the mirror you are bright
Fat girls cry in the dressing room
but you are skin pulled over bone

Poetic Sexploration

I have heard the term thrown around
ethical slut
overheard arguments in bars about its meaning
I just never knew
I've just been living
catching myself
connecting

1. Her sockwad penis and my puberty engorged vagina
2. Orange Liquor and lost virginity, I'm still glad I didn't bleed
3. Maroon boxers, a piece of gum
4. She was so incredibly soft
5. Half way through he was scared, his dad has HIV
6. Cheater, Cheater, Cheater, I guess me as much as him
7. Love explodes with my first orgasm
8. Set up by our friends in a room without condoms, I learned to give a blow job
9. I have taken virginity, she told me she had never cum like that before
10. He was so baby faced and we fucked all night on the futon in the shed
11. In between thrusts he sobbed, "I just can't do this" and "I want to do this"
12. There is nothing like the feeling of naked breasts upon an unclothed back
13. He was so nervous, so sweet, now I am the story to be told
14. Let me read your soul, only if I can read yours, a poet passing through
15. I wrote down a name and the details are lost in the night
16. Handcuffed together we walked home from a party it just made sense
17. Two at once, in the woods, in the house - they refused to kiss - I sucked a lot of dick
18. And then just the one, I don't think I can ever go back from big dicks, but I have

19. Love again, unexpected, porn, arguing - take down your hair - show me your tits

20. He told me to take off my dress because we are grown ups

21. Called in sick to work at Planned Parenthood as his dick was going in

22. Sweet secrets beneath the sleeping bag at the end of the new year

23. Neighbor boy who played Bob Dylan, his foot was in a cast, I love laughing during sex

24. Each other's little secret, she was a dream

25. A fifth of whiskey and late night tent set up - a friendship fling romance

26. One man, one woman, two blow jobs, he went home with me

27. OkCupid, we met, he rolled over after and told me he thought he was gay

28. A moment of mutual masturbation so divine

29. I WILL NEVER LIVE THIS ONE DOWN- BATMAN

30. We met on a porch, watched ourselves in the mirror and then he almost puked on me.

31. Could have been an orgy, 1 guy, three girls, cocaine, touching, kissing, I ran away

32. She ate my pussy all night after her husband came to pick up her sleeping infant

33. Maybe I have commitment phobia, over in two months, same position every night

34. The ginger-bearded metalhead boy

35. Justified cuming after 2 minutes, by saying I was just too beautiful

36. He smelt like trees-it was intoxicating-I didn't want to shower the next day

37. Two of the most beautiful women I have ever known

38. Snort this it's cocaine, no it's meth, no cocaine, no meth. 8 hours of sex

39. *Twin Peaks* and glasses of red wine, his cock was the strangest shape

40. A sort of kindred, a writer, he knew his way around a corset - shoved ecstasy up my ass

41. He brought me a book, a sweet gesture, a boring night in bed

42. A true friend, but we lacked the spark, I was his first one-night stand, Prince blared

43. I took the risk and invited him over, it wasn't the best or worst, it was meh

44. Dominatrix for a night, yes mistress, no you can't, I said "masturbate in that corner"

45. We came together every time and I let him shatter my heart three separate times

46. The Alaskan Hotel - a brothel in the 1800s, I lived up to its reputation, paying in cash

47. Only with men for the last three years, skinny dipping, my breasts took over our experience

48. Beautiful, she kissed me hard on the dance floor, I ate her out all night

49. A friend of a friend we exchanged graphic novels and orgasms

50. Drummer of the band in leather pants we ended up in his VW bus in the parking lot

51. White granny panties he never saw and a long walk home the next morning

52. Her kisses stayed on my thighs long after her lips left

53. He worshipped my body like only someone 10 years younger can

54. That kiss and touch in the photo booth was everything, she is so beautiful

55. Wordsmith with magic fingers in a sea of dick pictures

56. Tinder date gone poorly when he tried to guilt me for leaving after shit oral

57. She was so unlike women that usually like me and I felt so lucky

58. My Polish poet, he looked, touched, kissed, licked, and fucked like I was his prize

59. He helped me say goodbye to the United States with baths and tantric orgasms

60. Among his charming phrases *Of course I am a good lover, I have a French Passport*

61. Into his arms I was enamored with his cock, conversation, and orgasms

62. He had to prove that he has experienced sexism by having me suck his cock

63. My unexpected Highlander, he made me cum harder than any man has on the first night

64. After a terrible moment seeing my ex, she took me home and I squirted all over her face

65. Our friends thought we both needed it so they ran us a bath and pushed us in

66. I didn't want to be the first woman to tell him he was all talk and no follow through

67. I wish there was more to say, but it was really just that boring a night in bed

68. During a trip to Belfast we proved that hungover sex isn't always that bad

69. Missing all his front teeth, don't judge me, only a few thrusts in did I decide to leave

70. In between the eight rounds of sex we recited each other our poetry, it was amazing

71. Two months of texting after a tinder match and we finally met up, it was worth the wait

72. Worshipped my ass like no man before, still figuring out how I feel about him eating it

73. Not an English speaker, he texted, *What Up to I wish to take you from behind now*

74. He called me goddess and said my pussy was one of the most beautiful he'd seen

Fat Fetish

Some mornings I stand in front of the mirror
I look at the fat that hangs down from
breasts to waist to hips

I am Fat.

With number 2
I knew
what I was to him
Show me what you got girl
I didn't think you could move that way

With number 10
I knew
He pulled my hips into him and pounded from behind
Show me how you move that big fat ass girl

Some nights when I roll over in bed
I wrap my arms around myself
soft and fleshy

With number 20
He told me
He had watched me all night
I wanted to come home with you because
I have never been with a girl like you

With number 29
He knew I knew
You look like you could toss me around the bed
Would you like to?

Fetish is a form of sexual desire focused on a particular object,
body part

Fat   Curvy   Big Girl   BBW

With number 33
I don't think he knew
but he was awkward
almost uncertain of how to touch my vagina
but with eager desire in his eyes

With number 43
I knew
I had answered an ad
Seeking BBW for good night
I will treat you well

Do I make a fetish of myself?
   when I embrace my size
     when I am confident
or
am I simply a checkbox on the list of fetishes for men?

With 57
It was new to him
but as he says
You changed my whole life
I never knew how attracted I was
to women like you

With number 68
He was honest
Can you ride me?
Will you sit on my face?
I want all of your weight on me

Not all of them
but some of them

Wake Up

My lover and I quarrel in the morning
after the cheating and the fighting

> Down a long corridor
> a gauntlet of flashing films
> I am on an errand

You reach for me
stretch out your arms
kiss my neck

> I stand in front of a marsh
> becoming a desert
> becoming an ocean
> becoming a mountain
> becoming a jungle
> and then
> a slab of concrete highway

I turn away
I turn away
I turn away

I return to

> a washing machine overflowing with clothing
> soap spilling onto my feet

You were there
They were all around you
> You were kissing them all
> Every single one of them

  You

                                              standing on the front porch
                                              I drop the package in my hands

eyes glued shut with sobbing
you reach for me

I push you away
I push you away
I push you away

                                                              We fight
                                                              Scream

                                              You were kissing all of them
                                                         No I wasn't
                                              You thought that is what you saw

                                  Soap squishes under my toes

                          But I saw you
                                              You didn't see

anything
                          BUT I SAW YOU

Are you ok?

My shallow whimpering sobs continue
You pull me into you

I push you away

My lover and I quarrel in the morning
after the cheating and the fighting

Shameless

My friends and I sat around the kitchen table:

Remember that one time you let that guy do coke off your tits for free drugs?

Remember that time we drove from Bellingham to Portland with a rack of beer in the back seat and cocaine on the dashboard?

Remember that time you had a threesome while our other friend was asleep at the foot of the bed?

Remember that time we made the taxi driver take us through McDonald's?

Remember when you took that homeless guy home and fucked him?

Remember when you blew your hand up from a sparkler bomb and told the ER doctor it was a BBQ accident?

That time I babysat the kid and I probably shouldn't have.

Here is what happened:

I had spent a weekend camping

mushrooms, Adderall, Alcohol, and Insomnia

I had to work and couldn't get out of it.

My friend loaded a 9milimeter for me and told me to unload the round
    It will wake you up

Down the mountain I drove, stopping to pee and get a coffee. The six hours is a blur,

I needed ibuprofen and Gatorade, so I loaded the kid up in the stroller to 7-11.

I came to pushing the stroller down the sidewalk.

I came to with the kid jumping on me while I was passed out on the couch.

I came to while I was stirring macaroni and cheese on the stovetop.

I came to while I was peeing on the toilet.

I came to when the mom walked in the door.
Kid asleep next to me, TV blaring a Disney movie.

I am lucky she was understanding.

I came to when she and I smoked on the porch and she told me never to fuck up again.

Remember that time you were fucked up and still had to babysit?

Remember that time you puked out my car on the way to the airport?

Remember when you got sucker punched by that guys girlfriend?

Remember when we all got high on mushrooms and sat around topless?

Remember that time?

Her Tattoo

On my left side
On her right side
fingers deep within me
looking out there from her bicep
with piercing eyes
I know this shark
my eyes to
her eyes
I bury my face in her breasts
this is where I want to be
On her right side
On my left side

We Have Been Here Before

Around the table they stood
A cloud of smoke hovered above their conversation
Planning

Sharpies, paint, cardboard

My mom called me over

>*You are going to hold this sign*

Don't Take Away My Food. Don't Take Away my Home

>She read it aloud to me

Why? I asked

>*The man who thinks he is in charge wants to take things from us*

Why? I asked

>*Because he doesn't think we are important, and he loves money*

This is 1989.

>*You will hold this one too*

Women's Rights Are Human Rights

>She read it aloud to me

This is 2017:
My Uterus is Private Property/Keep Your Laws Off My Body/Love is Power/
Men Of Quality Do Not Fear Equality/Resist/Dissent is Patriotic
No One is Free When Others are Oppressed/Why is There No Maximum Wage
This is What the Revolution Looks Like/Respect Existence or Expect Resistance

Thoughts

Sometimes I think about what it would be like
to take that stranger home from the bar
and then I remember when I was drunk last night
I smoked a cigarette in my room and ate a bag of chips
and now there are crumbs and ashes all over my sheets

Sometimes I watch porn
my roommate suggested pornhub as a free site
be specific when searching he said
I type in:
Real lesbians fingering each other
Women getting spankings
Gay men making out
Women with pubic hair
Guys in dresses fucking chicks
Big dicks, medium sized tits
Pegging

Sometimes I wonder if I smoke so much
to give myself lung cancer
because I can't imagine living until I am old
so I light cigarette after cigarette after cigarette

Sometimes I look at tinder while I am pooping
wondering how offended someone might be if they knew
I hearted them while taking a shit
I think it means I am not that serious about it

Sometimes I start masturbating with extreme fervor
driving my fingers as deep in as I can go
and then stop
feeling too lazy
and think about how much easier if I had a dick
that would get hard, tug and yank, till I cum

Sometimes I wonder if I spend too much time
Pondering skinny women
Like what is it like in that body?
What is it like to go shopping and try on clothes?
Have sex? Eat in public?

Sometimes I think about all the gross things I do
how will I ever live with a partner
I think about when I picked my nose
Or farted in bed
Or smelt dirty socks and decided to put them on
And when I have eaten something off the dirty kitchen floor

Sometimes I wonder what I would do without
Xanax, Valium, Vicodin, or
really any pharmaceutical drug I have taken
to elevate a panic attack
I think it would be a hell of a lot harder

Sometimes I worry about all the nudes I have sent
my tits, my pussy, fingering myself, a dildo in
I have just sent them by text
but then I think I have received just as many dick pics
and I actually really like dick pics (solicited)
and I wonder sometimes if I am the only one
So really, I shouldn't worry that much about it, right?

Sometimes I imagine being a prostitute
Or a call girl or a lady of the night
How much money would I make?
Is there a niche market for a chubby bisexual woman
willing to do almost anything?
I think about how it would be such a good story
And I wouldn't have to date, and I would get laid all the time

Sometimes I want to be single forever

Sometimes I want to be married

Sometimes
        Sometimes

I think
       I think too much.

.

La Petite Mort

I took a day off to stay in bed and fuck myself

> I put phone away
> I put books away
> I closed the laptop

Bedside lamp on and naked

I cum over and over and over again at the touch of my own hand

It had been months since I needed to

I hadn't felt that urge till

I took the day off to fuck myself

I took my time

pushing in fingers first one
then two
 then three

> Pushing away images of other hands,
>   past lovers, or porn

alone

My little death over and over and over again
first hand
then toy

A strap-on dildo long ago placed in a drawer
                    Unboxed

> I took the day off to fuck myself

Single Judgment

Or why I swipe left
pertaining to men

Because you took a selfie from above while you were in bed and that is your first picture. All I can think is that you must be really lazy and are hoping that I will climb on top of you when we meet and want me to see what it looks like. I can't stop from my laughing and have had to set the rule that this is a swipe left automatically. Also, I screenshot them and send them to my friend.

Because you look like a douche bag. Like a really big fucking douche bag. And I know this needs some explanation. So it is because in your first picture you are out with your friends and it looks terrible, in your second picture you are in a suit with a bottle of some alcohol and then the last few you are posing with double thumbs up in front of a car, waterfall, or a group of women. Like seriously? Is this real?

Because my friend one time pointed out how a bunch of you look like minions, I have never even seen *Disciple Me* but I can't unhear what she said and now I fucking see it everywhere. I also screenshot these and send them to a different friend who is obsessed with how silly the little yellow guys are.

Because you used a snapchat filter. That is an automatic left.

Because you are so pretty, like really pretty and I get distracted thinking about whether or not you would let me put you in drag, but I also get super insecure because you are definitely prettier than me.

Because I have no fucking idea who you are, every single picture is more than one person.

Because you didn't write a profile description and I am forced to assume you are looking for someone just as shallow as yourself.

Because you took a gym selfie in the mirror, a gym selfie on a weight lifting bench, a gym selfie in the mirror again, and oh yeah, another gym selfie in the mirror but flexing and I just have to swipe left on that.

Because one of your pictures looks like a mug shot and I am slightly concerned it confirms a suspicion I already have that you might murder me. Because you look like you might have murdered someone.

Because I really in the end can't be bothered and because five minutes in I get bored and I think about how I would rather just eat some pizza and watch a film and maybe masturbate and because I spend so much time swiping left that when I do swipe right to

A) be immediately unmatched or
B) talk to someone for a few days and never actually meet

I realize the whole thing is a complete fucking joke and that pizza and masturbating is definitely better.

Family Portrait
In smoke

Mother

I was taught to make her coffee when I was five
the big red can of Folgers on the counter
six scoops to eight cups of water.
She needed it before we could talk.
At least two cigarettes and one cup of coffee.
She would silently stagger into the kitchen
pour her cup and straight to the porch
Sip, light, inhale, exhale

Grandfather

He has quit smoking now because of his recent stroke.
5 days in the hospital and they put a patch on him.
He started young, at least a pack a day
Marlboro Reds in quick drags, one after the other.
In his truck
In his shop
All over the property
The only reason he has really quit
is he can't remember he ever smoked.
His MS brain and three stroked brain won't let him.
He just can't seem to remember how he loved the quick
puffs.
Now when I visit I don't know what to do with him.

Me

I started smoking so I could lose my virginity with a boy.
I was 19 in class and he sat in front of me, he was
beautiful.
After class he would step outside, and flick click the lighter
taking long slow inhales that made me wet.
I followed him outside
bummed one

that night I bought my first pack.
Two months later we had sex.
Now I don't talk to anyone till after
Sip, light, inhale, exhale

For Gitana

Janis

Janis Joplin died in 1970

I saw a documentary one time
Maybe it was night train or midnight train or party train

The Grateful Dead on tour and Janis was there drinking
whiskey and singing

When I am most sad about the death of my friend, I
picture her there too

Animal

A lip that pouted out and away from the chin
Deep dark eyes
Dreadlocks
Then frankendreads and bangs
Then a bob
Was she like a cat?
Or a dog?
Sometimes a bird
Other times a spider

Juice

We joked all the time about holding an intervention
            for her juice addiction

Cranberry, apple, orange, pomegranate, mango pineapple
            If it was in your fridge, she drank it

We never had the intervention about what we really
needed to

I heard

Why did she think moving to Portland would help her get clean?
Heroin is everywhere down there.
I could have helped her.
Everyone knows people overdose there.

It was the only time I wanted to punch someone in the face

Fantasy

That she is here
That hawk on the highway with its wings spread was her
The whisper of *I am sorry,* and *I love you* was her
The crocus in the snowy ground was her
The ant that insisted on crawling on my leg was her
The song on the radio was her
The pull off the Southern Comfort bottle was her
The wind in a gust is her

Reprise

The Deception Pass bridge
The ocean below and ashes in hand
          all waters meet eventually
Sauvie Island
Topless walking into the Columbia and ashes in hand
          all waters meet eventually

Sometimes I feel guilty about the blue vial that sits in my room
ashes inside
but I cannot let go

For Adam

Jim

Jim Morrison died in 1971

We talked once about how we first heard The Doors when
we were young

About how the poetry changed our lives
and I told him about the t-shirts I wore when I was 13
and he had the same ones

When I am most sad about the death of my friend, I
picture him hanging with Jim.

Animal

Piercing eyes
contagious smile
A laugh that echoed for days
hair that flopped and flipped and swayed
sliding in front of the eyes sometimes
Was he like a cat?
Or maybe a dog?
Sometimes a hyena
Other times an ant

Pizza

Adam BigMcLargeHuge

It was the name he gave for online Dominos orders

I still use this name when I am really missing him

I heard

After he died, I looked at the string of posts to his Facebook wall

I wish I could have helped you brother
I had no idea he was so depressed
I wish we could have done more
I just never thought he would do that

I call my best friend and we talk about all the times

Especially when he skateboarded without a helmet down the biggest hill in town
Impulsive and rash
       he was always impulsive and rash, even in death

Fantasy

That he is here
The sound of skateboard wheels on pavement was him
The leaf that blows down from the tree was him
The snow that swirls around was him
That finch that landed right next to me was him
The song on the radio was him
A sip of a Stella was him
The wind in a gust is him

Reprise

I didn't get to go to his funeral

And sometimes I worry I never really dealt with it

Sometimes I feel guilty about how angry I am with his parents
      for never spreading his ashes
           for putting his belongings in a storage unit

I stare at pictures and remember
I am scared to go to the cemetery where his ashes are
         but I cannot let go

These are the names I have been called by men:

Cunt
Slut
Bitch
Whore
Stupid
Slag
Ugly
Fat
Disgusting
Girl
Crazy
Hooker
Hussy

Flirt
Shrew
Witch
Gross
Chunky
Massive
Poor
Trash

And by women too

I collect myself

in fingernail clippings
curly red pubic hair
the smell of socks
bobby pins in the carpet
popped zits
stacks of journals
skin tattooed

I collect myself
in case nobody else does

Things I wanted to tell you
(following our break up)

I am on a train to Portland and there
is a crazy cat lady drinking whiskey
telling everyone her cat always falls asleep
on the train, also, she is watching *Braveheart*

I typed and deleted this twice to
you today: I miss you, I still love you

You text me you are wrecked and it
makes me feel better, that I am not
the only one

I can't masturbate right now
touching myself just makes me sad
all I want is to be naked next to you

I am worried you might be drinking
too much to avoid your feelings, but
I'm relieved I don't have to deal with it

I washed my sheets so they wouldn't
smell like you, but tonight when I
crawled in bed I was mad that I had

I cried while at work today, big wet
silent tears. I thought about how you
say you've only cried three times
one of the times because of a steak
I laugh thinking of it, but I feel weak

I hate driving by your house, the
muscle memory of hand to blinker
still so strong, I want to turn left
into your driveway every time

I have been thinking about mistakes
yours and mine, how many we made
and if it really matters when things
didn't end because we fell out of love
when things ended for other reasons

My roommate says he saw you at
the bar and you seemed fine, Fuck You

I know it is stupid, but I miss your cat
your cat that isn't technically your cat
I miss your roommates, I miss a lot of things

Sometimes when I smoke on my porch I
think about the night I pressed you
against the door and made you cum
I think about all the times I made you cum

I saw our guy at the grocery store
today, the one who said he wished
he had a boyfriend so they could be
as cute as us. He asked how you are,
I said good. I didn't have the heart to
tell him we aren't together

I got Thai food today and laughed
to myself thinking about the
night I taught you about the big rice
noodles and the face of disgust you made
and how in the end you loved them

I am drowning in memories of you
each day they flood my moments
I am holding my breath to stay afloat

I really needed you today and I
fucking hated you for it

I listened to our album today in
the car, you were like a ghost
next to me, I could feel the weight
of your hand on my knee

I masturbated for the first time
today because I saw you and
we hugged on your porch
we hugged as we both grieved
for our lost friend
I forgot what your touch can do to me

We aren't talking right now
we tried, but it proved hard
I am not sure who more for
You would say me, I would say you

The Earrings

I have left behind during one-night stands in my 20s

I miss you

I am sorry I didn't come back for you

The vinyl record one
The metal with pearl
That curly one with red sparkles
The turquoise circle

You fell from my ear
                in the tussle of bodies
in the undressing from living room to bedroom
                in the hurried dressing of the morning

I left you behind

I miss you

That one my friend's mom made
The peacock leather feather one
The dangling silver one
The pin-up girl

Your matches hang in a row among the earrings that haven't
lost their mate

I wear these solitary earrings still, but I often think of you

The ones I left behind

I am so careful now about earrings

Our Noises

The knock
       knock of messages
              sent from sea
                     to space
                         and
                      then to land

The click
       of hotel door
              the drop
                 of heavy bags
                       and
                     the rip

of velcro

The sigh
      of ecstasy
          the moan
              of pleasure
                 the slack drop
                         of
                       body

          the silence

The whirr
       of bathroom fan
              the pounding
                of water against shower wall

        at 5 am

The breath
      the snore
         the toss

the turn
the groan
of sleep
the silence

The laugh
of the tease
the growl
of response
the heavy sighs
that know each
other

The beats
of hip-hop
the rush
of wind through car window
the flick
of a
lighter

the silence

these are the sounds   of you
and me

Wolves

Part One:

The woods behind her father's apartment had wolves.
They came from the darker woods
their howls in her ears as she tried to sleep
on the sectional nestled in the corner of a living room.

The air so chilled it caused her breaths to create quick
white puffs.
The wolves got closer.

It must be a different kind of woods to have wolves in it.
The pack of them nestled next to a fire singing their song
to the full moon.

There was a room of teddy bears and the child held her
mother's hand.

You can pick whatever one you want to

                                    The cop told her

                    Why do I get one?

                                    the curious child asked

Because you are special

                                    The cop told her

because you are special
because you are special
because you are special

There was a room full of instruments and the child held
her mother's hand.
It smelt of bleach and the whiteness was blinding:

white linoleum
white fluorescents
white paper on the table
white gown
white blanket draped across her lap

The child held her mother's hand.

white gloves on the doctor

because you are special
because you are special
because you are special

> *This isn't going to hurt*
> *Your mom is right here*
> *You are being so brave*
>> The doctor told her

The wolves always visited when she was at her father's apartment.

The howling in her ears as she peered out the window.

The window fogging now from the heat.

Part Two:

The woman has sex.
She is happy in moments of bliss and release.
He is 19.
She is 25.
She takes his virginity and they entwine themselves together in sweaty summer nights.
They wrap with one another on her bed in the attic.

And then she sees it
a flash

        Violent memory

She knows

        It was not wolves

A four-year old's mind sheltering her adult thoughts

You are not special
Because you are not special
Because you were not special

The woman does not stop pleasing her lover.
        It is a flash

        She wishes she had heard a howl in the distance

She is not special
But she is a woman.
Not the child.

She watches him dress in the morning.

First his boxers (she adores)
His white gym socks (to which she shakes her head)
Jeans (at least a size too big, as if he is unaware of his
slender form)
And one of those 80's animal shirts.

Woods. Wolves. A Moon.

You are not special.

Ancestry

in the mirror I am looking

for the shapes of ancestors
for living lineage of relatives
unknown to me

                                at me strange land eyes look
back from there
                                    half unknown to me
but I am finding home

In the soft lower lip of France
In the nose of Scotland
In the eyes of Ireland
In the cheeks of England
In the ear lobes of Germany

                                I trace these lines
                                there is no answer

strange lands in the curve of my face

                    face my of curve the in lands strange

I return to trace the line
I return to find a knowing
my face contains faces I
do not know
                                    both living and dead
dead and living both
you gave me my name
                                        my breath

your leaving became the start of my coming

In love

I lie trembling and quaking
                              on the bed
                                        splayed naked on sheets
blankets pushed to the floor

The breeze of summer cools the sweat on my forehead
The church bells down the road remind me there is time

My eyes shut
            my lover next to me
                              her arm draped across my
breasts
And
Clang
Clang
Clang
Clang
Clang
Clang
Clang
Clang
Clang

in the bliss
            the afterglow of
oforgasmonorgasmonorgasmonorgasmonorgasm
onorgasmonorgasm

I am in a world of no time
In bed, but I do not know it
Naked, but I do not feel it

I hear the bells
            the only ringing in my ears
                              the vibrations of my body
                                                        and
hers next to me

Gone

I can't send these texts to you
not now you are dead
                    but I still think of them
all the time
and even write them down every once in a while

OMG Gitana Mama
at a jazz club and
the singer is belting out
Amy Winehouse!!!
Wish you were here.
Xoxoxo

Dude, banged this
ridiculous punk poet
who would totally
annoy you, LOL
but he was pretty damn hot
I had to tell you

Ugh...so hungover
Just ordered a pizza
watching drag race
am still in bed
Wish you were here
Xoxoxo

Man wish you
Could go shopping
With me today. I need
Your brutal honesty.

Hahaha I just had
the most stupid day
it was all fucked
Call me later and
Let's chat about it
xoxoxo

I wrote about
you today. I figure you
would love it.

Don't be jealous
but I got a tat today
It is so awesome
Love you! xxxx

OMG I just saw
this woman who looked
so much like you.
But I mean of course
Not as pretty.
Love you bitch.
Xoxox

I feel stronger
Whenever I think
About you

Fuck. Fuck.
Fuck. Fuck.
I miss you so much.
Wish you were here.

I wish
I wish
I could send these

Passing

They talked in hushed tones
behind my back
when my friend died
>   *I didn't think she knew people like that*
>   *Do you think she has*

They don't know that

up my nose:
>   cocaine
>   meth
>   percocet
>   vicodin
>   adderall

in my lungs:
>   heroin
>   pot

in my stomach:
>   mushrooms
>   mdma
>   sassafras
>   ecstasy
>   acid

They don't know that
>   drugs have flowed in these veins

In the overdose of my friend I learned what kind of people do
drugs

and that I am not one of them

I wonder how it is I am passing?

If they knew I had been laced into a corset, bent over my bed, and had a gel capsule of ecstasy shoved in my ass before a dick.

How I am passing as not?

And what is it exactly I am passing at?

They don't talk in hushed tones behind my back
about my sex life

I have had sexual partners
more than 70
of all sizes
mostly smaller than me

I have not
known names
turned away from experience
hidden my exploits

What if they knew that I spent a three-month period of time fucking men I barely knew that I met online?

How is it I am passing?

I have not been called a slut

I have seen how few sexual partners it takes to be called a whore.

I wonder if

I am passing because I am fat